WHAT YOU ARE FOR

Inciting A Revolution In Your Soul

D0170299

MELISSA LA FLAMME

outskirtspress

DENVER, COLORADO

Outskirts Press, Inc.
http://www.outskirtspress.com

ISBN: 978-1-4787-5325-4

Outskirts Press and the "OP" logo are trademarks belonging to Outskirts Press, Inc.

PRINTED IN THE UNITED STATES OF AMERICA

Contents

FOREWORD

This volume is a shaman's brew of poetic ayahuasca. A vine of soul, of death, of new life. To just sit with these poetic lines and the power of the word, even if they jolt you or make you flinch, is in itself a breaking open of our egos, their compromises and identifications which bind us and hold us back.

You see, this is a new kind of poetry. What Melissa La Flamme offers, here, is medicine for the soul, and like an entheogen, gives you the needed boost to move out of your self-constructed cages. As you do that she baptizes you the Code Breaker.

In Melissa La Flamme's art of the written word there is no finished self; we are artist and artwork all at once; we are evolving mutants who must continually crack ourselves open, attuning to the poet's code-breaking notion to "let your heart break." Once we are fully alive with our broken open heart, the poet tells us, we can unfasten our passions and predilections to explore new territory as we evolve, love, and create a beautiful life.

Always, this book is ontological dynamite, a ceremony of soul initiation — which makes the reading simultaneously delightful and edgy, while Melissa's lines — always pushing the comfort zone of the ego and its false identifications and limitations the ego puts on itself. All this invites you to deconstruct yourself and encounter yourself anew, free of the old fear-based rules that hold you back. And Melissa does this with such love, encouragement and in joy. Do not let fear hold you back, is her great message as she opens you to imagine the impossible, as she calls you to dream big, and to subvert anything — like a surrealist — that suppresses the essential You that wants to express itself.

Melissa La Flamme shows you that even in the most heart-breaking ordeal, you may find meaning and hope in the initiation you are invited into through that heart-break. Above all, the poet calls you to remember what you are here for — your sacred purpose — that if nothing else gets accomplished but that, you have created the beauty you came to create.

Here we have shamanic poetry at its best, its freshest; a post-modern poetry that unites the old initiatory themes with crackling expressivity. Read — read and realize what you hold in your hand is not something to just relax with by the fireside, but is, itself a new-life-giving ceremony. So give that bad-girl and bad-boy within more room to play, express, and show your wildly creative power to cultivate what you are for and the life you came here to ravish. This is Clarissa on rocket fuel. Enjoy!

—C. Michael Smith, Ph.D., author of *Jung and Shamanism In Dialogue: Retrieving the Soul/ Retrieving the Sacred,* and the award-winning, *Psychotherapy and The Sacred*

ACKNOWLEDGMENTS

Many contributed generously to this book's first inklings and eventual birth; a process of years, perhaps lifetimes. Throughout the creation of this book, often it seemed it was writing me. This book insisted on its own birth, conceived in a dream. In one of those palpably real night-terrors, a huge, hand lunged at me through the darkness. Terrified, soaked with sweat, I knew it was going for my heart, to tear it out of my chest-cavity. Though I tried, I could not wake up, and in a semi-conscious state, I knew the dream was going to have me. In the morning, shaken yet enlivened by this dream image, a harbinger of soul, I re-entered the dream, and asked two questions that I often ask of dream images (and other beings and forms who come to encounter psyche): "What may I give you? How may I serve you?" With these questions, the otherwise ominous hand shape-shifted into an inviting, darkly feathered wing, now glowing. The darkly feathered wing opened slowly to reveal a message as if written in the palm of a hand: "Your heART," it said. I have come for your ART. And so this book was first blessed enough to be startled into the light by this insistent Dream invitation, a midwife for the initiatory medicine of the soul.

I am deeply grateful and indebted to my teachers, beginning with Paula Ehrich, my Open Studio Art teacher in high school, who shepherded a small group of us into the galleries of SoHo in New York City. There, she taught me how to see through the imagination-freeing lens of surrealism. To Shari Frausto, the first psychotherapist and "doctor of soul" to tend and care for mine, and to teach me, in the dangerous and dazzling trenches of psyche, how to do the same for myself and others. Thank you, Shari, for embodying how to catalyze a creative life and make soul. My teachers and classmates at Pacifica Graduate Institute, thank you for crafting a space for approaching the numinous through the art and practice of soul-making, for sending down the wisdom that helped my voice emerge through mythopoetic consciousness, out of the darkly shimmering recesses of my post-modern soul so that it may be of service.

Bill Plotkin and Mary Marsden, thank you for guiding me and twelve soul sisters and brothers into, but never out of, the wilderness of the American southwest, and down to the caves of psyche. Your fiercely loving, grounded support infused me with the courage to reclaim the sacred, vow to deliver the art I came to give, and do so as a continuous, sacred ceremony in service of soul and earth. To the deliciously real, beautifully-crazy-gifted soul brothers and sisters, with whom I meandered for a year — grit-covered, wind-tossed, sun-torn, and soul-stained — through the wilds of desert landscapes and conifer-kissed hills, we witnessed each other in the dark moonlight of the Underworld, you are in every word here, and I thank you profoundly.

To my friends, old and new, your support, love and fierce challenges have informed my voice as a servant-poet; thank you for showing up exactly when you did. And to Peder, long-time, forever friend of my soul, once my husband, graduate school classmate, anam cara, thank you for everything.

To my family, especially, my Mom and Dad, Phyllis and Bob, and my sister, Tracy, along with my ancestors, particularly my grandmother, Nonna; all of you wove into my heart the feel of richly textured and supportive love, empathy and awe, faith in the sacred, commitment to hard work — the ancient threads of a rogue tapestry of soul in which this book comes wrapped — in my cells you live and in my heart you are always. My loving gratitude to you, Mom, Dad, and Tracy, is boundless.

To Michael, for feeling into every word in this book with me, offering solid feedback and confirming reflections, reading every poem with a writer's nose, an artist's soul, and a fiercely open heart. As this book gestated, your loving support held me through its final quickening — encouraging me to tap the healing agent in the excessive and consciousness-altering voice of surrealism. In this fecund reciprocity we make, your steady care helped me to deliver my soul's gifts of service to others. This book would not be what it is without the love you unleash on me. With everything in my heart, thank you, baby.

Special thanks go to teachers I have not met, but have studied and reveled in, drawing immeasurable inspiration and guidance. Among them are artists, philosophers, writers, psychologists, anthropologists, mystics, poets, healers, and all-round Troublemakers: Carl Jung, James Hillman, Thomas Moore, James Hollis, Marion Woodman, Sylvia Brinton Perera, Steven Aizenstat, Maureen Murdock, Bill Plotkin, Joanna Macy, Stan Grof, Timothy Leary, Clarissa Pinkola Estes, Lynn Andrews, Marija Gimbutas, Robert A. Johnson, Joseph Campbell, Jean Houston, June Singer, Otto Rank, Alice Miller, Starhawk, David Whyte, Mary Oliver, Adrienne Rich, William Stafford,

Rainer Maria Rilke, Frida Kahlo, Jim Brandenburg, Jackson Pollock, Andy Warhol, Diane di Prima, John Keats, Allen Ginsberg, Lawrence Ferlinghetti, Pablo Neruda, Antonio Machado, Carlos Castaneda, Dante Alighieri, Jelaludin Rumi (and modern translator Coleman Barks), Robert Bly, Susan Griffin, Pierre Teilhard de Chardin, Salvador Dali, André Breton, Cy Twombly, Anais Nin, Joan Didion, Donald Hall, Jane Kenyon, Sam Keen, C. S. Lewis, Alejandro Jodorowsky, Terence McKenna, Henry Miller, Martin Prechtel, Maria Sabina.

To the community of my followers and friends on Facebook, you were among the first audience for the poems in this book. Thank you for your gracious reception of my work from the outset. As these poems emerged fresh from the mythopoetic oven, I was terrified to share them, but had no choice; the poems insisted. From there, the Conversation you and I carried on and the ones you had with each other confirmed for me that my work itself was calling out to be shared more widely. Your generous support and enthusiasm lifted my courage to write and wherewithal to publish with the hopes that the medicine these poems carry is healing for many — for humans, more-than-humans, for the earth, and the soul of the world.

PROLOGUE

When you live from your intuitive core, your belly, your heart, let your soul lead and spirit guide you, your words and actions will be naturally subversive.

You will go to your edge. And there, you will not be alone.

Question is, will you wholly inhabit your own revolution? In beauty? This inner revolution is a perpetual ceremony of the heart. It is what you are for.

When you are real, cooked down to essence, rather than half-baked to get approval, to look good, the projections from others may fly, seek you out and try to stick to you. Don't let them. Instead, let your authenticity support you in carrying on whole-hearted, vulnerable conversation to resolve whatever arises. It is hard work. Uncomfortable. Deeply human. Can be harrowing. And often downright delicious. Intimate. Naked. Courageous work marked by your solid presence. Here. Now.

I'd rather be whole than good, C. G. Jung said. And by whole, he meant real, messy, ensouled, deeply human, heart-broken open with compassion flowing first to ourselves, to resource and prepare to let it flow widely, to others.

Being too comfortable, amenable, pliable to the point of contorting yourself — is a ticket to selling your soul right up the river. Don't buy it. When you live from your own knowing-ness, from your gut and your wildly-rooted intelligence, you feel alive. Genuinely, madly, creatively alive.

Being real — true to your Self, your soul — is gritty. And grit causes friction, makes fire to clear the way for living a revolutionary act. This act is marked by action that the earth and the soul of the world are crying out for. And the cry is going to get louder, more pain-filled, and grievous before enough souls answer wholeheartedly.

When you get real, it is actually not about you. Your individual program is only the ground from which you step. From which you step and choose whether you will make this life of yours a walk of grit and beauty, or one of accommodation to the forces that insist you do it their way, be well-behaved, produce, consume, make nice, and as the poet, Mary Oliver says, "barely breathing and calling it a life."

Thing is we're not talking a self-improvement project; that's only the gateway. We are being used. By Spirit. One way or the other: we go consciously or we are abducted — individually and collectively, now. So it's a great time to dive in.

When we realize we have no choice but to offer ourselves up — like a sacrifice — to the mystery of Great Spirit's guidance, this guidance insists on shaping us as a soul-centered contributor. And we're in it! Soul's got us. And Spirit carries us along. We're goners to those egoic, mechanistic, competitive ways; the ways that have undone the earth and so many souls who walk the earth, swim her waters, send roots down into her and watch from the skies.

To inhabit your own core, your vital, knowing center and a soul-centered way of being, you need to do the inner excavation.

What we call, in Jungian psychology-speak, Shadow work and in shamanic-speak, Underworld soul work, including ego-dismemberment work to heal old wounds and retrieve parts of your soul you had otherwise disowned or split off. We need these pieces of our souls, as well as aspects of our bodies, and our connection with Spirit, and with the earth, along with the Other-than-human-ones and wild intelligent forms of life — to feel deliciously alive, ready to roll, to serve this crying earth and love 'em up.

This is real adult work, asking everything of you. And will alter your world completely, but before that happens you'll be met with severing old ways, dismemberment, metaphoric death, dreams, visions — both lovely and horrifically heart-pounding, yummy, gut-wrenching, Beauty, raging tears, sweet snot, broken open heart, blue-shimmering darkness, warm, comforting light. Rebirth. Love. Hope. A deep sense of connection with it all. And a palpable knowing of what you are for.

So it's a slow dive, a conscious descent into the depths of your soul, the dark ground of your being and your dreams: the Underworld of your psyche. This is vital work — no way around it — to discover what you've tucked away in the archetypal Shadow of your own psyche. If you're lucky you will unearth what you had otherwise disowned to adapt to the egoic, mechanistic, competitive, earth-ravaging ways of modern Western culture. And most often, these pieces of your otherwise whole psyche that you had disowned are what makes you utterly You. Beautifully. Creatively. Wildly alive. Authentically so. You. And you are needed here.

Your essential soul's powers — what you were born with before you lost track of them and they, you — are to be found there, in that excavation into your dark depths, awaiting you to carry them home, like mama leopard carries kitties. With a fierce tenderness, knowing that all life — yours, your beloveds, the earth, humans and other than humans — is at stake. The world needs you to be fully alive. Real. The world needs you to find, bring home and embody your soul's gifts and healing powers. It's messy work. It's what we are for.

When you are transparent, you will stand out as you are truly seen. When you are transparent, others can "see through" you into you as your heart and true essence shines. You are clear, direct and kind. You are not an enigma; you don't leave people scratching their heads wondering what you just said and did.

You do not hide. You are honest to the bone. You are courage enfleshed.

When you are congruent, you are wholistically aligned. What you think, say, feel in your heart, feel in your body and the actions you take line up to support and reflect each other. You know it in your body, often in your gut, when you put your attention there.

Congruent. Authenticity happens in the guts and bowels of your life. Being authentic is the grunt-work of the soul, of any deeply human, spiritual path. Being half here, half there, half-hearted, faking it to look good, strategizing to make things easier for your self — that's the common way of the unconscious clotted middle, driven by our egoic, addicted culture.

It's a way that lacks wholeheartedness. Lacks real courage to let the heart break. Shatter. Broken whole and holy open to finally know compassion for self, others, earth. To live and love — on-fire, fully alive, juiced and ready to serve.

Being authentic and soul-centered costs you your ticket to ride from the collective mainstream to the illusion of safe and secure. And opens the door to your bloody and glistening, broken whole heart — reveals to you the honey of this wildly delicious, messy life. Leaves you and those you touch, feeling radically free. Without choice now. Solid and light. Authenticity strips away all that is NOT real. All that is not made from love, to love. All that is of enriched soul and inspired Spirit remains. There is no living a soul-centered life without being authentic — without mustering the courage to do the excavating in the dark: the Shadow work.

Again, C. G. Jung: "People will do anything, no matter how absurd, to avoid facing their own souls." [1]

What will you do?

1. Carl Jung, Psychology and Alchemy, Page 99.

INTRODUCTION

You have to be mad, don't you? Ravishingly mad to let your heart break. Ravishingly mad to let this poetry take you, like a lover. And yet, this is what you are for — to take yourself to your edge where you will find you are deliciously human. Where you will ignite your own natural-born powers to incite a revolution in your soul.

Let these poems be an invitation to conceive the nearly impossible: to let your heart break. Break wide. Break open. Yes. That. I know. It's okay. Listen: it's what you are for.

With your heart splayed open, glistening to fully inhabit this one throbbing life, you are fully here. This is what you are for. And the world is waiting for you.

If this calls to you, then walk with me along a meandering, wild path into this verdant forest of poems fertile enough to start a new life within you. Here, you will find a furry and musky collection of words and images born of longing, the soul's suffering, the heart's ecstasy as it emerges from heartbreak and downright earthy bliss, rent from the human spirit and the soul-birthing canyon lands of the American southwest.

Immersed in the desert of southern Utah, in May 2013, where these things are said to happen, where winds whip up a hot springtime and custard-colored sand sticks to sweaty skin, I offered up my heart to the fierce desert wilderness to be broken again and again. Best thing I ever did. Rather than invest one more drop of my vital energy in any attempt to avert the inevitable, this tremulous move dropped me into what I am for, into sharing this book with you.

It is astonishing, isn't it? How much energy we expend trying to keep our heart from breaking? Thing is, it's wasted energy. And worse, it keeps you distant from your depths, your core, your animal, natural humanity. From every one. From every thing. We're meant to be broken. To shred. Melt. Burst open. Come into compassion and exquisite empathy and love for every thing. This is what this poetry is for.

The world is screaming for you to let your heart break. To be fully human is to let your heart break. Over and over. To not deny it when it happens. To mend it when you can, when the blood stops flowing. I know; that's bewildering. And I invite you; be beWILDered. Be deliciously human. The 19th century poet, Rainer Maria Rilke suggested, "let everything happen to you — beauty, terror; just keep going." [1] And the contemporary Buddhist teacher, Pema Chodron tells it like this: "Lean into it...Let the hard things in life break you. Let them affect you. Let them change you. What is the lesson in this wind? What is this storm trying to tell you? What will you learn if you face it with courage? With full honesty and — lean into it?" [2]

Let it rip you open. Tear your eyes away from distraction, and turn you toward the thresholds that beckon you. The ones that matter because they know that grief is the doorway to Love; the step into crystal. Into expansive, generative, natural, sweaty, more-than-human-including-human love and purpose.

Don't ask me how. Mystery knows how. I am a servant-poet. I will tell you this though: you may come to a no-choice place. And there, you may find utter freedom in that no-choice.

Seems that the world is begging us to let the breaking happen now. Within. To mirror and heal the breaking happening all around, without. We are being asked to break. Break Up. Break down. Break out. Shatter. Bleed. You're on the right track now. The right track to break into radical loving like a thief hungry for soul, ready to serve sweet, dark humanity and the earth's tangled questions that insist we return her urgent call to let our hearts break into compassionate action.

These poems are intended to offer you potent and sweet medicine, both a soul-soothing elixir and soul-arousing juice to help heal the heartbreaks of your life, and ignite the wildly transformative fire in your belly. The very fire that is stoked by the hard times that often drive us to our knees, shake us down with a velocity that produces the impact that affects a "break down." Stay with me, now; we're almost through to the other side: and so, with our full attention and unruly grace, the "break-down" may become "break-through," and shift us from outmoded and no longer enlivening ways of encountering this one life into a wholly reorganized way of belonging in the world that is generative, creative and organically wild — juiced and ready to go. This is what this poetry is for.

This way is radical. A deliciously alive, broken, open heart is a revolution. And it is what you are for, as a human being. Like this poetry, your torn open, glistening heart — is a wild, throbbing portal to aliveness, to living a life with your own freaky artistry. Imagine that.

Imagine, this poetry is a doorway to Mystery, to raw creativity in-born in you, waiting to be fully birthed into your one life. When that happens, an evolutionary intelligence rips through your heart, takes root in your life, and opens you to a juicy, natural way of thriving in sacred reciprocity with every thing and every one. This is what you are for.

May this poetry move through you like water and wind shape the red rock canyon lands of the American southwest, like your own heart shapes the soul of the world — not forcing and not holding back.

Melissa La Flamme, MA
Denver, Colorado
May 14, 2014

Notes:
1. Excerpt from "Go To the Limits of Your Longing," by Rainer Maria Rilke, *Book of Hours I*, translation by Joanna Macy and Anita Barrows. 1996. Riverhead Books, Berkeley Publishing Group. New York.

2. Excerpt from *When Things Fall Apart: Heart Advice for Difficult Times*, by Pema Chodron. 1997. Shambhala Publications, Boston

CHAPTER 1

WHAT YOU ARE FOR

To imagine the impossible is deeply human.
To re-member every
thing is alive,
dreaming, intelligent,
coming for you
to ravish you awake
is your inheritance.

To muster the heart
to stretch to the edge of what beckons you
is your ticket to ride.
This is what you are for.

Your cellular capacity to imagine —
unbound —
is a subversive technology,
altering
every thing
through an evolutionary,
fractal spin,
juicy with
elemental creativity.
Dangerous.
This is what you are for.

Let your self be
claimed
by darkly-feathered
unchained hands,
servants on a mission,
come to take you
hard
down to the wet caves
of what flushes your delicate skin,
dampens your palms,
wakes you like a raging
dream
into shimmering
forces
unknown.

Here, you will know
you have no choice.
Finally
free,
you submit
to the way that has called you
before speech.
This is what you are for.

Let this Trouble
take you
to your knees.
With your sweaty, full attention,
wrapped in the limbs of the sacred,
kiss

the plump, pink lips
of your tender
soul.
But wait.
This is not about you.
You are being used.
By every thing.
This is what you are for.

Now, draw into
your being
the throb
of the one way of belonging
that is yours to make matter.
This is what you are for.

The broken-hearted,
glistening hum of
your taut, tangled
body will give
off a fragrant, unruly
intelligence beyond the Machine's measure
of right, wrong, reason.
This is what you are for.

Have you come here to make Trouble
for Assurances and Security?
For Greed and Convention?
For Routine and Predictability?
For Comfort?
Good.

Those are the Killers of
what you are for.

The planet is
erupting with
Uncomfortable.
The earth is writhing in pain.
Feel her suffering in your blood, your bowels, and
you will know what you are for.
Taste compassion for the sacrificed,
the slaughtered and
you will love like the Milky Way.

Shatter your old ways, and
show me how
your soul blushes
alive with arousal.
This is what you are for.

Be an unpopular harbinger,
an endangered one;
a tender, firmly sprouted
sentinel of
the rhizome of archaic revival.

Do not take a seat.
She is ready for you.
The soul of the world
will see you now.

What have you come to give her?

CHAPTER 2

BE ART NOW

Those brilliant shards
of the sharply
reasoned, respectable,
socially acceptable
good-girl,
good-boy
pieces of your world?

Go ahead.

Scatter them
while you can.

Before they harden into
a mosaic you think you have to
call your life.
Before their cutting edges become
too comfortable.
Too safe.
Too grey and small.
Too tightly
bound in a modern,
exacting,
soul-extracting
realism —

in a form
not of your own making.

You know what I mean.
Shake loose while you can.
It's alright.
We are here.
Walking on crystal,
on a path —
more like an edge —
wholly, holy
unknown
til now.

Unfasten.
Be what allures you,
moistens your waiting mouth,
lights your wet, wondering eyes.
Become
the musk in the fur
that makes your
smart-girl, smart-boy
quiver with the vulnerability
that is your birthright
to embody;
the bad-boy beauty
at the fringes of
imagination,
the bad-girl whisper
in the landscape of your sweaty
Dream.

WHAT YOU ARE FOR

The surreal door of
your soul's
authentic
workshop
opens
when you unfasten
those heavy, culture-bound
hinges they welded
to your heart.

Flung open, now, ready to melt,
it is love that you craft
with fire and blood
of the earth.
Life that is artistry. Your one, true
freaky way.
Beyond that door,
on holy ground, you are.
Welcome.

The slow
approach to your artisanal
edge to deliver the cargo
you came to bring
is what will
lick you alive.
This sacred edge is
your luminous, custard-colored
stomping ground.

This edge beckons one
rare move.
Simple as it is,
it asks everything of you —
if you would follow, now,
the invisible bend
on that darkly scented trail. If
you would only
be art now.

CHAPTER 3

HEY, CODE BREAKER

What program
beneath the program
holds you
back from becoming
a solid evolutionary?
An artful leader of
your own soul's
movement
to
set
you
free?

You need to retrieve
the Code Breaker.
The one who knows how to
operate
in your depths,
reveal to you
through the trap door, under
the fabric of the culture of media-driven,
sociopolitical, economic strains, under
the skin of the relationships that no longer
serve soul, under

that which mutes the colors of your
healthy living,
creative
loving,
passionate
serving.

An initiatory act of rebellion
is a subversive maneuver to
take heart
while it shatters the old code.
To lean into hope,
to make love
from the repurposed materials
of your tender life.

To live with courage even in its absence is
to live authentically especially when
it costs everything.
To free yourself enough,
to heal yourself enough
from the effects of the culturally-mastered
virus; the Diabolical Hacker of your soul.

Time to re-set your organically beautiful, wild
system of body, mind, heart and soul.
This is the underground
work of freedom.
Messy.
Uncivilizing.
Scary.

Sexy.

To free your mind
to submit, holy embodied
to the fire, the one
oddly kindled
by your glowing fears, the fears that
keep you from realizing —
I mean fully realizing —
that so-called reality in which we move
is a pre-fab construction
by what poet, Diane di Prima, calls the Metal Men;
the ones who pull the levers
to keep you enslaved, paying taxes,
ingesting poison,
consuming, shushing
your Dreams and killing
the earth.
What the fuck, right?

The work that often derails the hearty evolver
is the move into your fears
of rejection
by people you know
who do not want to be free,
who will not join you in evolution,
who may even try to undermine
your heart's desire
to be fully alive.
And then, there is
the fear that you might go

bat-shit
crazy if
you are free.
Yes? But listen:
these fears are the allies
of the Metal Men.
They count on you
to feed them.
Do not.

When you're ready
enough,
reach up
through the rubble with your
dusty, blood-stained hand, and
with all you got,
answer the call
from the Code Breaker.

Soft like honey you will become, sweet and potent,
companioned by Vulnerability and Courage,
flanked by No-choice
but to dive hard into your artistry,
your freaky-true way of serving —
serving your soul and others — severing
with a sharp, large blade
your familiar, habitual, and
outmoded ways
of being accepted by others,
but not loved
by yourself.

WHAT YOU ARE FOR

If you take this way,
you will know
it is the one you can wholeheartedly choose;
the only one that wants to ravish you
open;
take you apart, scare you sacred,
shake you
down,
make you
human to re-member
you
came here
to be free.

This way,
the one that appears
through the crack in the rubble;
the one that says, This Way to Mystery;
this way through to the door with the unfastened
hinges to the Unknown,
darkly sparkling life-sources, gifts
with no shortage of delivering deliciously
artful madness.
This way
to
freedom.

My prayer is this:
That you embody
your sweaty-palmed-longing to rave —
with soul as freedom's teacher and

Spirit as bad-ass trail guide to lead you
to the know-how in your shattered, open heart.
The heart
that knows gusty winds and Spirit's
downpours
do not last.

The heart of you,
reverent now, having kissed
Death's evolutionary
intelligence —
licks life alive again, giving birth
to screaming rebellion,
to the freedom to
give it all back to
the crying earth.
To pay the only debt we owe.

CHAPTER 4

DARK-WINGED VOW

Vastly open
Desert-Love,
I am calling you.

With this one voice,
rent raw,
soul, gooey,
stripped to shimmer,
I lay down
this fragrant vow.

You call me
in Dream
after tremulous Dream.
You claim me.

Splayed in soft
surrender to your harsh,
custard landscape,
stoking honeyed
desire to let melt
the ground of my being
into yours.
I submit, salivating,
anticipating the wild,

hungry ones come
to carry me off.

What ways does Mystery
live in
the sweet, dangerous crevices
of my darkening, dusty skin?
Another question
to romance, to inhabit
while tracking ancient ones who
move to insistent
throbbing drums, calling me
home
to the invisible hum.

Desert-Lovers, Moon-Weepers
on the trail,
tracking you.
You, Ocotillo.
Desert Lavender.
Jumping Chollah.
You, Milky Way.
White Sage.
Coyote Canyon.
You, Cougar Creek.
Creosote.
Red Rock.
You, Ragged Wash.
Mountain Goat.
Setting Sun.
You, Grandmother Moon.

You, Fragile Sand.
You, deliciously alive,
broken-open
hearted one.

Gathered sweat, mustering
sinew,
bodies
grown ripe from
carrying land song,
unearthing archaic prayer,
pulsing in
the under
ground of Dream.
Torn up to bone.
Down, ripped hard to runny.
Ravished by Darkness.
Warmed by outrageous
hope, without
knowing what for.

Soul of the fecund,
the animal body,
the anima mundi
come to re-collect
a debt, a vow
to Mother.

She said,
You, Smoldering One.
You, come to

romance the sticky
Dream
of the feral
heart of
everything?
You.
With life at stake,
kiss me.

You, Desert-love.
I kiss you deeply,
slowly —
Mother
Father
Brother
Sister
Lover.

I kiss you
like a dark-winged vow made by
my never-not-broken
whole
heart,
shattered
open
as a glistening sacrifice
to the blood of tomorrow.

CHAPTER 5

IN YOUR LOVE

In your love, my body
is ecstatic, my soul
seduced by the
brush of your
warming, pollen-sparkled air.

Your unquestioning, courageous
touch teaches me
the way true
love lives, in the cells
of our common blood;
in the soul, we embody.
In the way we risk our names.

You take me
back to that darkly-feathered
hand; the one that came for
my glistening heart
insisting I give
art;
that I give everything,
seducing
from me a vow
to romance
the soul of the world.

A vow, you promised would cost
everything.

I kiss you deeply. Again.
As I enter the softening
ground of the medicine
land of you; the land of
my deliciously alive, shattered
heart, you
work my tender,
sweaty body, rip me
open to receive
crystal shards of your teachings,
come to shred
ancestral layers,
sticky with outmoded cellular code,
invisibly carried,
trying still — beyond my devout knowing —
to give the slip
to this honeyed artistry.

I apprentice to the sacred
seduction of you.
You,
the one;
the love I was born
to make.
The only vow I came to keep.

You,
Red Earth, forgive me.

Red Rock, reverent,
I am your
lover.
Scrub Oak.
Sugar Sunshine.
Crazy-blue, orange sky.
Bird-song sweet.
Red-tailed Hawk.
Owl.
Quiet Mountain
Lion.
Pink quartz.
Hogback.
Foothills.
Soft, dry wind.
Matted, wild grasses.
Underground Spring, feeding
Cottonwood,
thirsty with knowing how
newborn Cactus
re-member my vow.

Ripped raw, I am
re-calibrated by the sacred
approach to you on my belly.
The same way I approach a sacred
wound.

You have seduced art,
from my once distracted heart,
fierce love, from my once terrified body —

you know how to reveal my soul,
shakedown my walls, melt my eyes.

Take me,
make me your mythic
servant-lover. You,
with darkly-feathered hands,
loving eyes of art light.

Trembling,
tear-soaked,
I vowed to
romance you, knowing
that loving you asks
everything of my
aroused animal
body, my sweaty
servant-intellect.
My heart,
obliterated.

I know of no other true way
to offer my broken heart,
open to serve you than
to submit
to the mystery of this romance —
to let the honey flow from my
tongue
into your open
river mouth.

Here, I feel how the soul of the world
has been stripped raw,
needing a new word for ready.
Ready for a whole-cloth re-write of
our collective, tragic
romance with you.

I am your pen;
use me to deliver
your impatient invitation
to sacred reciprocity.
To the place
where you wait for every one of us
to muster the courage
to risk ourselves,
on bended knee,
in this mythic, reverent
romance with you.

In your love,
I find the courage
to dip the archaic pen
of my inheritance
in the blood turned
liquid gold —
the medicine
of your wound
and mine.

In your love,
I use this instrument

of the sacred,
quivering with earth's
embodied intelligence
to romance
the soul of the world,
to love you.

I am your servant-lover.

Seduce me.

CHAPTER 6

A LONGING TO INHABIT

Listen.
You,
Tender One.
You,
Raving, Reverent Soul.

You,
what do you long for?
How do you call its name?
Listen for how
it calls yours?

Have you let yourself
kiss those sacred
lips?
The ones inviting
you into the conversation
that matters.
Insisting on this reverent
raving as your birthright.

That's right; your birthright,
and not some wild-ass
luxury.
What you long for

is your sacred
responsibility
to inhabit.

With devout and not too precious
attention, give yourself
to these questions.
To this longing.
Give yourself
like a lover.
Like a tender, baby-green shoot gives
herself to
new growth, unspoiled
by names.

Like this,
witness your fiercely fragile
longing,
while Mystery holds you,
while the world holds you
when you thought
you were forgotten.

Like this,
your longing will ravish you,
and now,
you must ravish back.

When you do,
your soul will walk you
to the soft, thirsty ground

of your being.

Sink in.
That's it.
All the way in
to a lush, furry landing.
Lose your mind there.
Sing to rocks,
seduce pine trees, make love
to long
grasses, warm
red
earth.
Rave
reverently.

Inhabit your longing,
and know that songs like this
are sung to carry you,
inhabit you
til your song
sings you.

You must let them.

CHAPTER 7

DANGEROUS

Artistry is subversive
like generative love.
Like vulnerability.
Tangled in the
nourishing roots
of the sanely creative
human.

Dangerous.
Inducing underground
movement,
artistry and love run amok
against the cultural current
that wants you,
YOU
in line,
to work,
on time,
paying
your
taxes,
buying more shit,
destroying the planet.

Because, you see,
your natural-born
freakylicious
artistry — as a way of life —
upends
your membership to the Cultural
Consensus Club.
Downright ousts you from
that meeting with Nonsense
that threatens to
cut you off
from your
instincts to live
your true inheritance
as this gorgeous, unruly
creature of
flourishing,
seminal
intelligence.
Here now,
to be used
to serve
what throbs,
imminent,
alive,
whispering
your name – beckoning
you
to do what you came for,
you Freaking Artist, You.

CHAPTER 8

RAVISH

When that dark,
soul-kissed Dream
comes to ravish you?

Take you hard
in the night
to your depths?

Let it
have you.

It's not a matter of whether
you will go
on a deliciously terrifying descent
to your own soul's
liquid,
penetrable
depths.
It is a matter
of how you will go.

Will you go willingly?
Submit to Mystery?
And not only in some sweet
surrender, but
in utter, truly human

submission,
splayed, laid
out for the taking by the Other
of your Dream?

Will you
take the elegant
dive into the unknown
of you, into what is Other-than
you, to tear you
open to shimmer?

Only from that darkly
sweet place will you know
the earth
and how she cries,
how Mother
waits for you
to Dream.

Or maybe
you will resist.
I get that.
Then maybe,
you will be abducted.
I get that.
That's what most of us do, see?
It's what we do until
we don't.

The abduction by your Dream
to carry you to

your soul's promising lap
is the more
harrowing
approach to the numinous,
the luminous
tremulous truth
beckoning you —
the terrifically human way
to go
down
beautifully
in a hard-banking dive
into the
eye-rolling, yum
of You.

Let the Dream
have its way with you.
Take you like
an ecstatic lover
come to rip alive
your throbbing,
heart.

This is your invitation
to drench
your life with the wild blood
of your Dream.

CHAPTER 9

PRAYER-KISSED

I kiss deeply, slowly,
the open mouths of bewildered souls,
who without wholly knowing
yearn to drink the raw,
live waters I offer.

A sacrament of honey-fire,
spread like the wings of a prayer,
poured from my broken
open heart
into yours,
to kindle your soul's smoldering longing
for everything
real, natural.
Human.

You are drawn in, captured
by the strong scent of your own soul's persistent
ache for spontaneous combustion of your true life.

Allured,
scared sacred,
you are slayed.
And I am here,
with you, loving

in this aching, shimmering humanity;
as the core of you opens,
giving way to your own essence
to reveal the quiet seed of you
that waits to bear the ripe, full fruit of
your artful soul.

You are beckoned to a numinous, impossible thirst
for that barely-known danger of being
terribly, beautifully, madly alive,
stripped bare to the ground of your being.

Here now, to live in
your glistening, raving
heart,
vulnerable, ravished, undone and messy
in a world where anything but
is accepted
as the safe way
to belong.

CHAPTER 10

FALL

This is not
an endurance event.
This is an
unraveling, gorgeous
sweaty adventure.

If it feels like hell —
with no purpose —
then stop.
Stop.

Feel into your heart,
drop down to your knees,
learn to pray
your way.
Listen to what your soul
can hear and your head insists
you do not.
Listen and stop denying what you
knew before they told you
what to think, how to feel,
who to be.
Listen.
Ask questions,
give no answers.

Stop indulging the fantasy
that misery — or some half-life
is your destiny,
your penance,
your humble inheritance.
It is
not.
It is the path
of culture-bound fears.

Your unruly courage
asks you to make love
with your own heart.
To take — like a lover —
your inheritance
is to claim
what makes your soul
warm and runny,
what makes your heart drip
with desire to thrive,
what opens your psyche,
your body to ecstatic states,
what beckons you to inhabit
wild artistry —
artistry enough
to kiss alive
the gifts they told you
to stuff away.
These are the gifts you carry.
Like a mother, carries child.

WHAT YOU ARE FOR

The timing is ripe.
The opening invites
birth now.

Your soul will catch you,
Baby,
when you
fall.

CHAPTER 11

FRAGRANT SACRIFICE

Some wounds
will not let go.
They have not come for that.

What pains you,
shapes your soul,
has come
to claim you,
call you
to your knees,
instruct you,
induct you,
reveal to you
the elixir in your heart,
the Mystery in wilder, natural
ways, in the ways
they taught you
to turn from,
to fear.
To snuff.

You see,
the medicine
in your fundamentally

dangerous
human
capacity to imagine, to expand
into ecstasy, shatter, melt into
prayer,
when everyone
is looking,
calling you
crazy?

That medicine in
those wounds insists you
let yourself
be crazy,
Beautiful One.

Let these wounds
teach you how to be
beautifully
human —
unleashed, animal,
embodied, snarling,
spitting,
laughing,
praying,
exalting,
making
fucking
noise
enough

to save your
soul,
to prepare you
to love
the earth and
the Others
who came before,
are here now,
and will come later.

That is what these wounds are for.
These wounds are Initiators.
Beauty-makers.
Some say, Troublemakers.
I say, same thing.

Let these teachers
initiate you
on the terrifying ground
of what undone
smells like.

Let these teachers
show you how
to ravish the sacred
nature of your being.
And then,
give it all
away.
Make it sacred,
sacrifice

what has kept you
small, safe,
sweet and good.

With this song
of sacrifice,
I lay down
this sweaty
prayer,

this invitation
to submit to sacred
terror,
salivating,
anticipating the wild ones,
the hungry, come
to carry you off,
take you
to ecstasy
in the breath
of the divine.

Gather now,
mustering
sinew,
bodies
grown ripe from
carrying land song like
archaic prayer,
tears
pulsing in

the under
ground of Dream
in landscape
verdant beyond
the Machine's measure.
Allied,
torn up to bone.
Ripped hard to warm and
runny.
Ravished by Darkness.
Shiva, Shakti, Durga,
Gaia,
Pachamama,
Ashpamama.

Warmed by outrageous
hope, without
knowing what for.

Soul of the fecund,
the animal body,
the anima mundi
come to re-collect
a debt, a dark-winged
vow
to Mother.
To Beauty.
To Love.
To this luscious,
animal

WHAT YOU ARE FOR

body, come
to give away

this fragrant
sacrifice
for the blood of tomorrow.

CHAPTER 12

HOLY HACKER

The yet to be born ones want to know

what makes your reasonable,
respectable, socially acceptable
safe self
squirm?

What makes your good-girl,
good-boy
stir uncomfortably?

Stir and squirm
with a hidden
desire
to inhabit
your birthright
to the vulnerable
authentic art
of you —
the art of you that writhes
alive when you live
in the fertile landscape
of the fiercely tender
heart of you?

WHAT YOU ARE FOR

Yes.
Right there.

The heart of you
that knows being real,
saying what you mean,
seeing it through —
is dangerous
these days.

But look,
they are waiting
for you to be
what juices
you,
what shakes
and slays
you
after the suffering
melts you,
re-organizes,
re-shapes you,
after Beauty
clears the ground
of your being,

and tears opens your heart
to a fractal
kind of loving,
a revolution
of the sacred.

Will you let your soul
ravish you right into
the belly of Spirit?

To be reborn.

The yet to be born ones
want to know:
will you kiss deeply
the gritty ground
of Mother
risk your self radically
and learn how to call them Home.

Call them
with a song of wild loving.
Hold that sweet note
in your blood-stained hands,
as you romance
this artisanal
dangerous
edge
of you.

The soul-defining
edge,
that one rare move,
marked
by a darkly scented
lure—
a lure that

cries for your courage,
courage,
the ancestors
installed in you.

Courage,
the yet to be born ones
wait for
you to unleash
like a holy hacker's code
on your own soul,
on a culture,
that has forgotten

how to love.

CHAPTER 13

THE MEDICINE

Every artist,
the artist in every one of us
came here to create,
to be created,
to contribute to the intensely
infinite gallery of all life.

To create a life
that is loving, solid in serving,
shimmering in complexity,
alive in beauty, healing in love,
rooted in piety,
no longer afraid to say,
pray.
No longer afraid to say,
God.
Ready and walking
through the door
with the unfastened hinges,
the misty light to worlds
waiting, to intelligences
creating, come to heal,
to ignite hope in you,
again,

to deliver trust to you,
like an infant placed in your care,
trust
in your own goodness,
your own power
to claim your art,
your one messy life and
make it beautiful,
to pray it down
into the heart of God.
Prepared to act,
accountable to the art
that names you.

From this place,
you feel it:
you are being used
to carry a gift
of creativity
made
pregnant
by the darkly sparkling
Dream that shapes
your humanity,
the Dream
born of an archaic
wisdom that
waits for you
to muster
the life-giving prayer

of your tender heart,
your natural-born,
crazy-intelligent power
to give away
the art
you are,
as a servant
of the love you are,
as an apprentice
to knowing:

love
is the Healer.

God
is the Medicine.

ABOUT THE AUTHOR

Melissa La Flamme, M.A. is a visionary artisan of cultural evolution, author, poet, shamanic guide and teacher, Jungian psychotherapist, depth psychologist and troublemaker. Melissa lives in Denver, Colorado serving souls — humans and other-than-humans — worldwide through soul-arousing poetry and writings, as well as provocative spoken-word performances, shamanic counseling, healing and teaching grounded in depth psychology, archetypal psychology and Jungian psychotherapy. Melissa kindles souls' smoldering longing for everything real, natural and deeply human to teach us how to track the soulful scent of that persistent ache for spontaneous combustion of our one true way of inhabiting the heart of the soul of the world.

Visit her online at www.jungiansoulwork.com and on Facebook at www.facebook.com/MelissaALaFlamme.

Printed in Australia
AUHW011443060720
330370AU00004B/87